THIS BOOK BELONGS TO

IF YOU LIKED THIS CONTENT
LEAVE ME A GOOD REVIEW.
I THANK YOU
VERY MUCH

YOU CAN FIND ME AS
NATY BOOKS

www.ingramcontent.com/pod-product-compliance
Lightning Source LLC
Chambersburg PA
CBHW060530010626
45794CB00023B/3113
* 9 7 9 8 8 7 0 8 5 0 9 0 0 *